From the author

The ten years or so I've spent teaching Aboriginal students in remote schools have provided me with the most treasured experiences of my life. The one frustration however, has been the endless search for reading material that will capture the hearts and minds of my students.

If little children are to value reading, the words and the pictures must first reflect a little of themselves and their world, their dreams and their imaginings. For many young indigenous readers, the world of shopping malls and party dresses and pet parades portrayed in school texts is far removed from their primary experience.

Children in remote communities live deeply textured lives shaped by the sights and sounds of the bush and nurtured by the warmth of close family bonds. These children are young adventurers — tracking lizards across the drifting sandhills, finding food in bush and tree and earth, camping out under starry skies, catching the mail plane to town for the weekend ...

This book is for those children. Most of the poems were written to support literacy programs in my classrooms and the content was shaped by the young people I taught. Not all the experiences are happy ones and not all are universal for indigenous children. Children from the following schools helped shape these poems: Palm Island State School (Queensland), Ltyentye Apurte, Yipirinya, Alekarenge and Canteen Creek Schools (Northern Territory) and Rawa Community School, Punmu (Western Australia).

I am indebted to Jenny Taylor for agreeing to take on this project as illustrator. Her humorous and sensitive contribution surpassed all my expectations.

I also wish to acknowledge Vanessa Nampijinpa Brown whose wonderful poster 'Sad Boys are Sniffing' inspired the poem *Sad Boys*. I am grateful too for the valuable support and insights offered by the Pitjantjatjara and Warlpiri students at the Institute for Aboriginal Development in Alice Springs (where I worked for several years). Malpiya Heffernan and Joan Heffernan offered advice on content during translation lessons and Margaret Mary Turner also provided valuable comment and encouragement. Pamela Nangala Sampson, Jessie Simpson, Pauline Nakamarra Woods, Rachael Jurra and April Napaljarri Spencer taught me much about culture, language and friendship.

Jill McDougall

This book is dedicated to Isabel Taylor and to the students in the bush schools

Jenny Taylor

Anna the Goanna

and other poems

Written by Jill McDougall
Illustrated by Jenny Taylor

The bike ride

I had a bike
I really liked,
It had no brakes,
It had no light,
The chain was loose,
The gears were tight,
But hey!
It went like **dynamite**.

We had a race
From P.J.'s place,
And I went first
With heaps of pace,
Past the clinic,
Past the store,
Past a dozen dogs
Or more.

I kept my lead
And picked up *SPEED*,
Doing ninety —
Guaranteed!
I chucked a wheelie
On the turn,
You should have seen
That rubber burn!

Then at the grid,
I did the skids,
In front of all
The little kids.
My chain flew off,
My wheels got bent,
I lost my seat,
But off I went.

At the creek
My legs went weak,
I couldn't move,
I couldn't speak.
My bike took off
On the wet cement,
She gave a shudder
And in she went.

Now my bike
Is a deadly sight,
It has no chain,
It has no light,
One wheel goes left,
And one goes right.
All I need
Is some **dynamite!**

Going hunting

My father goes hunting for turkey,
My brother goes hunting for toys,
My mum and my nanna,
Go hunting goanna,
But sister goes hunting for boys!

Anna the goanna

Anna the goanna
Is fat and slow.

Her belly is like jelly,
Wobbling to and fro.

Here come the hunters
Looking high and low ...

Go Anna, go Anna,
Goanna, go!

Sleep

Goanna likes to sleep
In the sandy ground,
In a soft warm hole
Just a little way down.

Crow likes to sleep
Near the starry sky,
By a big bird's nest
That's way up high.

I like to sleep
In a cosy bed,
With a blanket for my feet
And a pillow for my head.

Wake up!

Wake up! Wake up!
Here comes the day.
Look! The sky is
Pink and grey.

Now the sun
Is getting higher,
Wake the kids
And light the fire.

Make your dad
A cup of tea,
But leave enough
For you and me.

Let's go hunting

Fe fi fo fum,
Let's go hunting with our gun.

We'll shoot a roo,
With a .22.

Get him on the truck,
With a bit of luck.

Stir up the fire,
With a piece of wire.

Chuck him on whole,
With a heap of coals.

Chop off his tail,
With a rusty nail.

Have a good munch,
With a crunch, crunch, crunch.

And finish off our supper,

Smart flies

I don't think most flies
Are too clever or wise.
They get stuck in your ears
And they crawl in your eyes.
They dirty the windows,
They dirty the wall,
And they don't seem to have
Any manners at all.

But I do think our flies
Are the smartest around.
They can crawl up a wall
Without sliding back down.
And if you decide
To go walking outside,
They'll sit on your back
And enjoy a free ride.

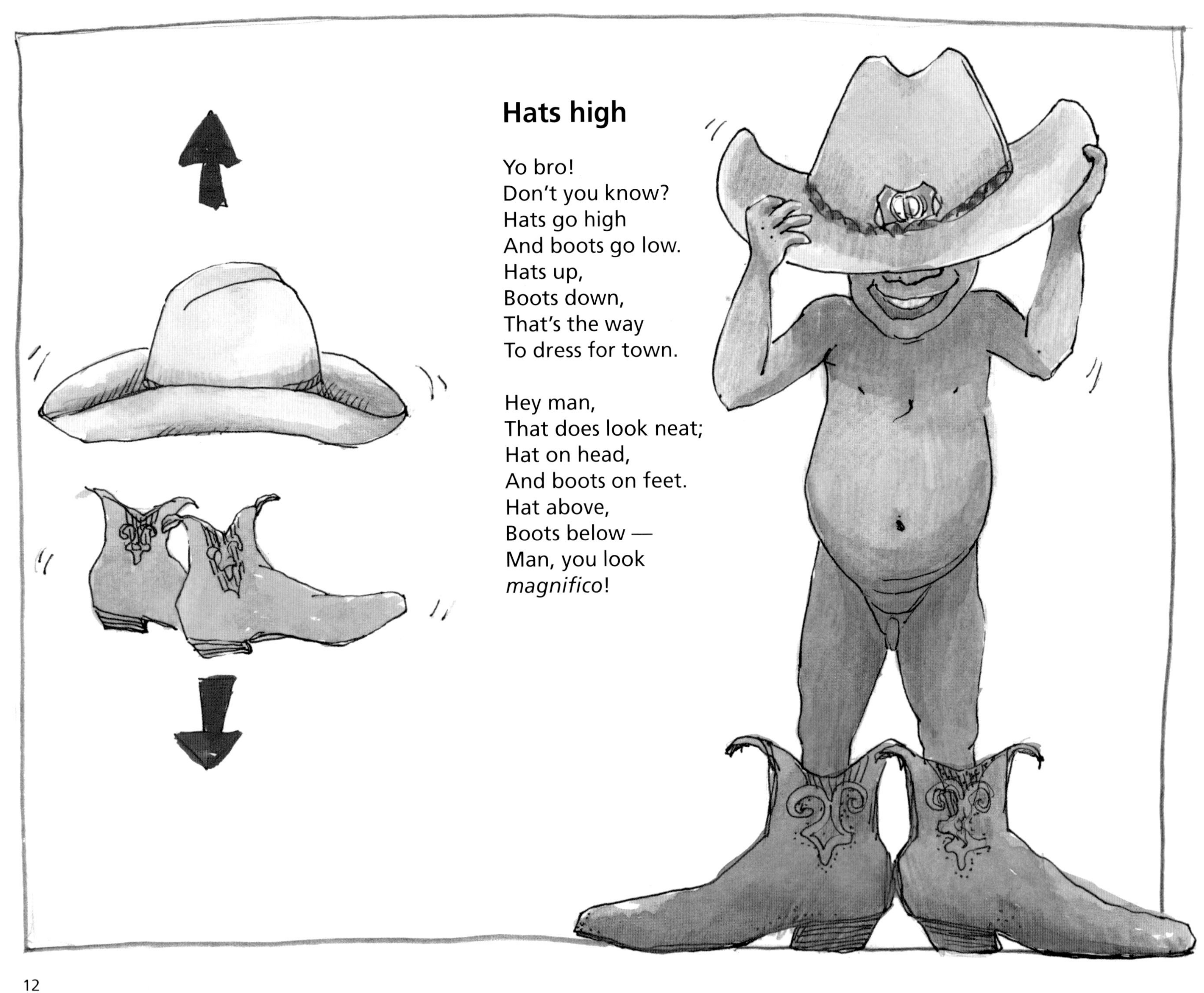

Hats high

Yo bro!
Don't you know?
Hats go high
And boots go low.
Hats up,
Boots down,
That's the way
To dress for town.

Hey man,
That does look neat;
Hat on head,
And boots on feet.
Hat above,
Boots below —
Man, you look
magnifico!

Baby talk

Babies talk
In baby voices,
Making funny
Little noises.

Babies don't ask
"How are you?"
Babies just say
"Goo, ga goo".

When you ask them
How they are,
Babies tell you,
"Ga, goo, ga".

Babies talk
In baby ways,
But who knows what
They really say?

Fire!

Old Kangaroo and his mate Cockatoo
Were travelling south,
Where the icy winds blew.
As night came around,
They found some flat ground,
In the shade of a cave where the river gums grew.

"It's freezing down here,"
Grumbled Old Kangaroo,
"But I'll make a good fire
To warm us right through.
I've never seen trees
As enormous as these,
I'm sure I could find us a big log or two."

So into the bush
Hopped Old Kangaroo,
Straight to the place
Where the biggest trees grew.
He was back in a while
With a HUMUNGOUS pile.
"This is great," said his mate, "'cos I'm shivering too."

Then Old Kangaroo and his mate Cockatoo
Fetched small sticks and big sticks
And old sticks and new,
They even took leaves
From the bushes and trees.
"This will soon warm our bones," laughed the triumphant two.

As the fire came alive,
The old fellows threw
More branches, more logs,
And a giant tree or two.
Way up on high,
They could see the sparks fly.
"I'm feeling much warmer," said Old Kangaroo.

Then down from the ranges,
A little breeze blew,
And it whistled and whined
Through the trees as it grew.
Soon everywhere
In the hot smoky air,
Sparks from the roaring fire floated and flew.

"Now I'm (ouch!) much too hot,"
Complained Old Kangaroo.
"Well my feathers are melting,"
Cried poor Cockatoo.
And as a fresh breeze
Carried sparks to the trees,
The two silly friends were beginning to stew.

"BUSHFIRE!" At last cried one of the two,
"Everything's burning!
What are we to do?"
But try as they might,
It was too late to fight,
For feathers and fur were burning up too.

Yes, feathers and fur
Were burning up too —
Nothing was saved
As the fire roared through.
All the birds and the bees,
All the bushes and trees,
All the creatures that lived there had perished there too.

* * * * * * * * * * *

Many years later, a young kangaroo
Was travelling south,
With his mate cockatoo.
They stopped at the scene
Where the fire had been,
And decided to camp where the river gums grew.

"I'm shaking with cold,"
Said one of the two.
"Let's have a fire
To warm us right through.
I'll get some sticks,
And a few little bits,
We don't need too much —
Just a small fire will do."

Five little lizards

Five little lizards,
Sitting on a log.
One jumped off
And was chased by a dog.

Four little lizards,
Sitting in a tree.
One jumped off
When she swallowed a bee.

Three little lizards,
Sitting on the wall.
One jumped off
When he heard his mother call.

Two little lizards,
Sitting way up high.
One jumped off
'cos he thought he could fly.

One little lizard,
Sitting on a shelf.
"Dum-dee-dee,
There's only me"
She sang to herself.

One scary night

The night was dark and spooky,
And the wind came whistling round.
The fire was slowly dying,
When we heard that dreadful sound.

It was not a dingo calling,
It was not a midnight owl,
It was like some creature full of pain;
An eerie, chilling howl.

We stared out at the darkness,
Wondering what could be there.
The shadows of the branches
Danced like fingers in the air.

My father said, "You kids sit down,
And everyone be quiet!"
He grabbed his rifle and his axe
And walked into the night.

We all crept closer to the fire,
Our faces big with fright.
Tall shadows flickered up and down,
Like phantoms in the light.

Then we heard a shuddering moan
And a crunching of feet on the leaves.
Something behind us was moving in close
And its smell wafted through on the breeze.

The footsteps moved closer and closer,
A revolting stench filled the air.
I felt as if long icy fingers
Were crawling around in my hair.

BANG! We heard in the stillness.
CRASH! Then a thump in the trees.
An aching groan split the darkness,
As something fell to its knees.

Our eyes burned through the blackness,
Desperate to focus and stare.
What was lying in the bushes?
What had been walking out there?

Then one of the trees seemed to shudder,
A giant black shape breaking through.
Silently it approached us,
And bigger and bigger it grew.

"Dad!" We cried as he reached us,
We raced to his side in a flash.
"What did you find in the darkness?
What was that bang and that crash?"

"Let's go and see," said my father,
Giving my shoulder a squeeze.
So we all held hands in the darkness
And together we walked to the trees.

First we saw where the branches
Had broken and cracked as they fell.
The leaves had been crushed and trampled,
But worse was that horrible smell.

thump
thump
thump
thump
BANG!
CRASH!

Holding our breath, we moved closer,
Not daring to utter a sound.
Then we stopped, as we all peered together,
At a place on the shadowy ground.

A tremor went through our bodies,
A groan from our lips filled the air.
That terrible smell still lingered,
But nothing, no nothing, was there ...

Mighty mosquito

I'm a mighty fat mosquito,
And my friends all call me Moz.
I drink fresh blood three times a day,
Because … well just because!

Some frothy blood for breakfast
Is a great start to the day,
And if I'm super hungry,
I'll get more to take away.

A warm blood soup for dinner
Is a mozzie's true delight,
And if I'm in a party mood,
I'll whine and dine all night.

Today I'm truly famished
So I need a snack attack,
Just a little from your belly
And a bit more from your back …
Yum!

Now I'm a mighty fat mosquito,
Even fatter than I was.
So don't you mess,
Oh, don't you mess,
No, don't you mess
with
the
Moz!

Ozzie the star

I'm Ozzie the Mozzie,
Muscley and mean,
I'm a street-fighting,
Back-biting,
Drilling machine.
You might not see me coming,
But you know when I've been,
'cos I'm Ozzie from the Mozzie
Olympian team.

Yes …
I'm Ozzie the Mozzie,
Athletic and lean,
I'm a low-flying,
Death defying,
Stunt machine.
I believe I'm the greatest
The world's ever seen,
And I'm the star of the Mozzie
Olympian team.

Flies in disguise

Flies, flies,
What a surprise!
There's all sorts of flies,
In every disguise …

There's green flies, there's blue flies,
There's teeny-weeny new flies.
There's real flies and toy flies,
And little girl and boy flies.

There's mummy flies and dad flies,
Away-from-home-and-sad flies.
There's ugly flies and cute flies,
And munching-on-my-fruit flies.

There's speedy flies, there's slow flies,
There's big buzzy blowflies.
There's lazy flies and slack flies,
And-always-on-your-back flies.

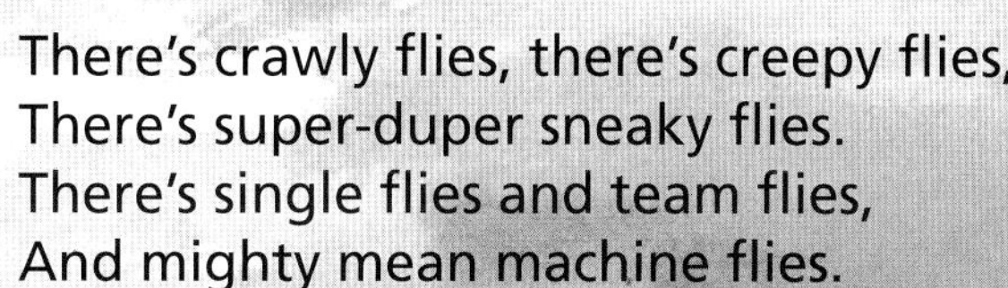

There's crawly flies, there's creepy flies,
There's super-duper sneaky flies.
There's single flies and team flies,
And mighty mean machine flies.

There's glider flies, there's flutter flies,
There's on your bread-and-butter flies.
There's house flies and horse flies,
And floating-in-your-sauce flies.

Flies, flies,
What a surprise!
There's all sorts of flies,
In every disguise.

Tin cans

I had a tin can full of sand,
My brother had another.
We pulled them up one side of the hill,
And raced them down the other.

The mail plane

Listen up! What's that sound?
Is that the mail plane coming down?
Hurry please,
And get the keys,
We're going to catch a ride to town.

You go first and get the gate,
Quickly now, we can't be late,
Run ahead,
And shake a leg,
The pilot isn't going to wait.

Now what's that up along the track?
Must be the cattle coming back.
You get out,
And give a shout,
Then scram before the bulls attack.

The ground's a little boggy here,
We could get stuck with all our gear,
But never mind,
You get behind,
And push until you've got us clear.

At last we've left the muddy ground,
I can't wait till we get to town,
I'll buy you clothes,
And videos,
And a BMX to ride around.

Tomorrow we'll see Auntie Sue,
And all the mob from Yuendumu,
We'll get a snack,
At Hungry Jack's,
And catch the bus at half past two.

At last! The airstrip's down this lane,
Across the grid and past this drain,
You grab the swags,
And all the bags,
Now here's the mail but …
WHERE'S THE PLANE?

Going home

Well there's me and my ma,
And my cousins in the car,
On the track outback,
Where the wild things are.
The cockatoos are crying,
And the desert oaks are sighing,
As the sky turns scarlet
With the day's slow dying.

And my aunties (all three),
Have been waiting for me,
And they stir up the fire,
And make some hot tea.
Then we jump into bed,
When the kids are all fed,
Snuggled down safe and sound,
With the stars overhead.

Crow

Crow, crow,
Where do you go,
When the day gets dark,
When the sun sinks low?

Crow, crow,
I want to know,
Do you rest in your nest,
With a little pillow?

Crow, crow,
Yes or no,
Do you do a little somersault
And hang by your toe?

Crow, crow,
Tell me if it's so,
Do you sleep with your little ones,
All in a row?

Crow, crow,
Please don't go,
Tell me where you sleep,
When the sun sinks low.

Growing things

All through the nights,
And all through the days,
Different things grow,
In all different ways.

Flowers grow taller,
Stems grow longer,
Bees grow busier,
Perfume stronger.

But plants grow weak,
As the sun climbs high,
Leaves grow limp,
And the soil grows dry.

Birds grow silent,
As the day grows old,
A liquid sun
Turns the sky to gold.

Shadows deepen,
A restless breeze
Sends a message of hope
To the trembling leaves.

Black clouds hustle,
The night grows longer,
The wind grows wilder,
Fiercer, stronger.

The heavens rumble,
The sky grows bright
As streaks of lightning
Split the night.

The sky sends a sprinkle,
The wind grows still,
Flowers grow hopeful,
As tiny drops spill.

The rain grows heavier,
A waiting flower quivers,
Puddles grow to boggy holes,
And boggy holes to rivers.

Then the flowers grow grateful
As they drink their fill,
The heavens grow silent,
While the world grows still.

Honey ant

Group 1: Honey ant, honey ant,
Where do you sleep?

Group 2: (*On hands and knees*)
I sleep in a tunnel,
So dark and so deep.

Group 1: (*Taking a step forward*)
Honey ant, honey ant,
What's on your back?

Group 2: I carry sweet honey,
Around in a sac.
(*Moving backwards*)

Group 1: Honey ant, honey ant,
Don't run away.

Group 2: My children are calling,
I really can't stay.
(*Moving backwards*)

Group 1: Honey ant, honey ant,
Why run and hide?

Group 2: Your teeth are too sharp,
And your eyes are too wide!
(*Running off, chased by Group 1*)

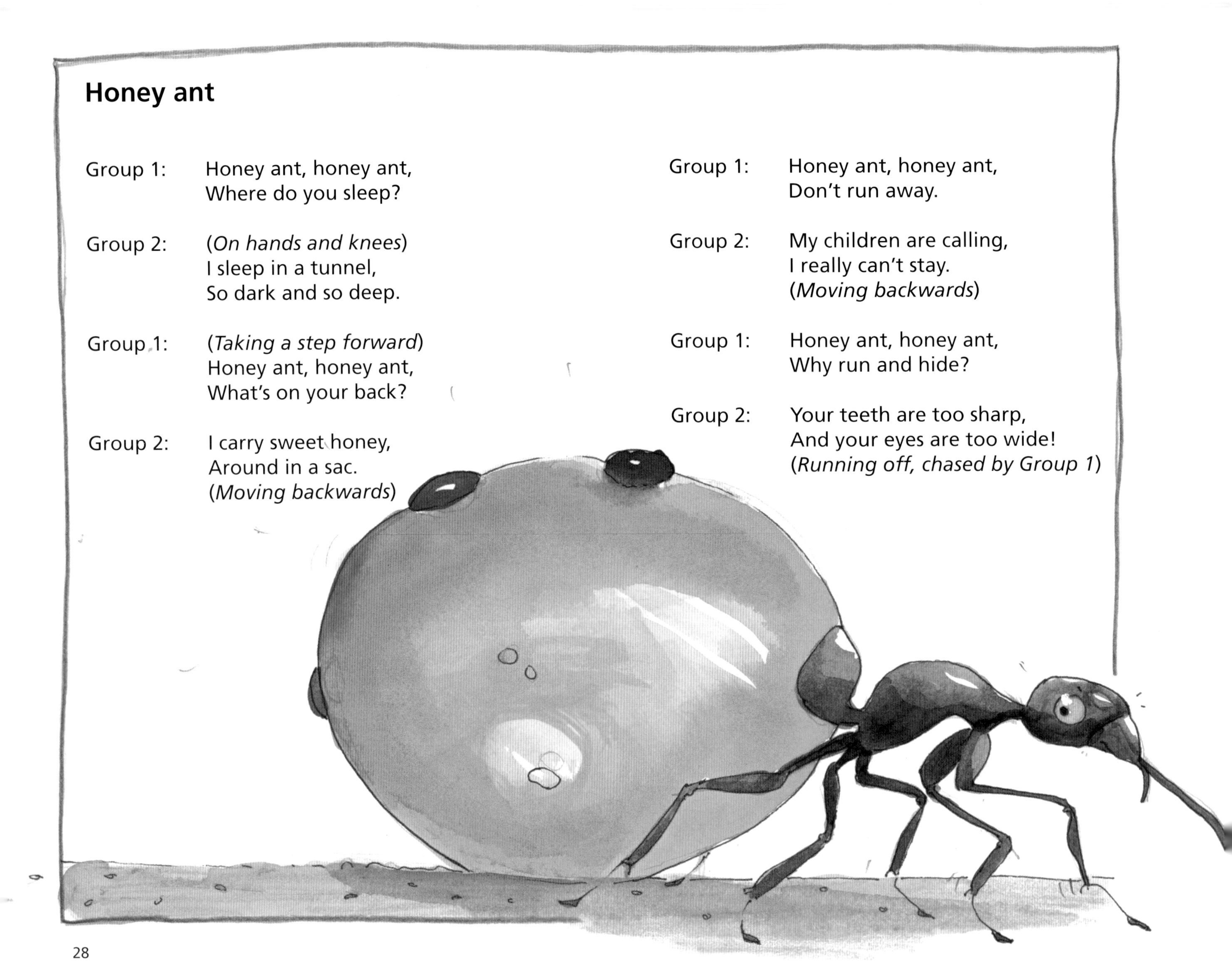

Snake

(*Very quietly*)
S...s...snake is very slippery,
S...s...snake is very quiet,
Silent as a sliding shadow,
S...s...snake is out tonight.

S...s...snake is coming closer,
S...s...snake is smooth as ice,
Slipping down the silvery sandhill,
S...s...snake is out tonight.

(*Increasing tempo*)
Down the sandhill, through the bushes,
Hunting frogs and hopping mice,
SNAP! She's found her slippery supper,
S...s...snake is out tonight.

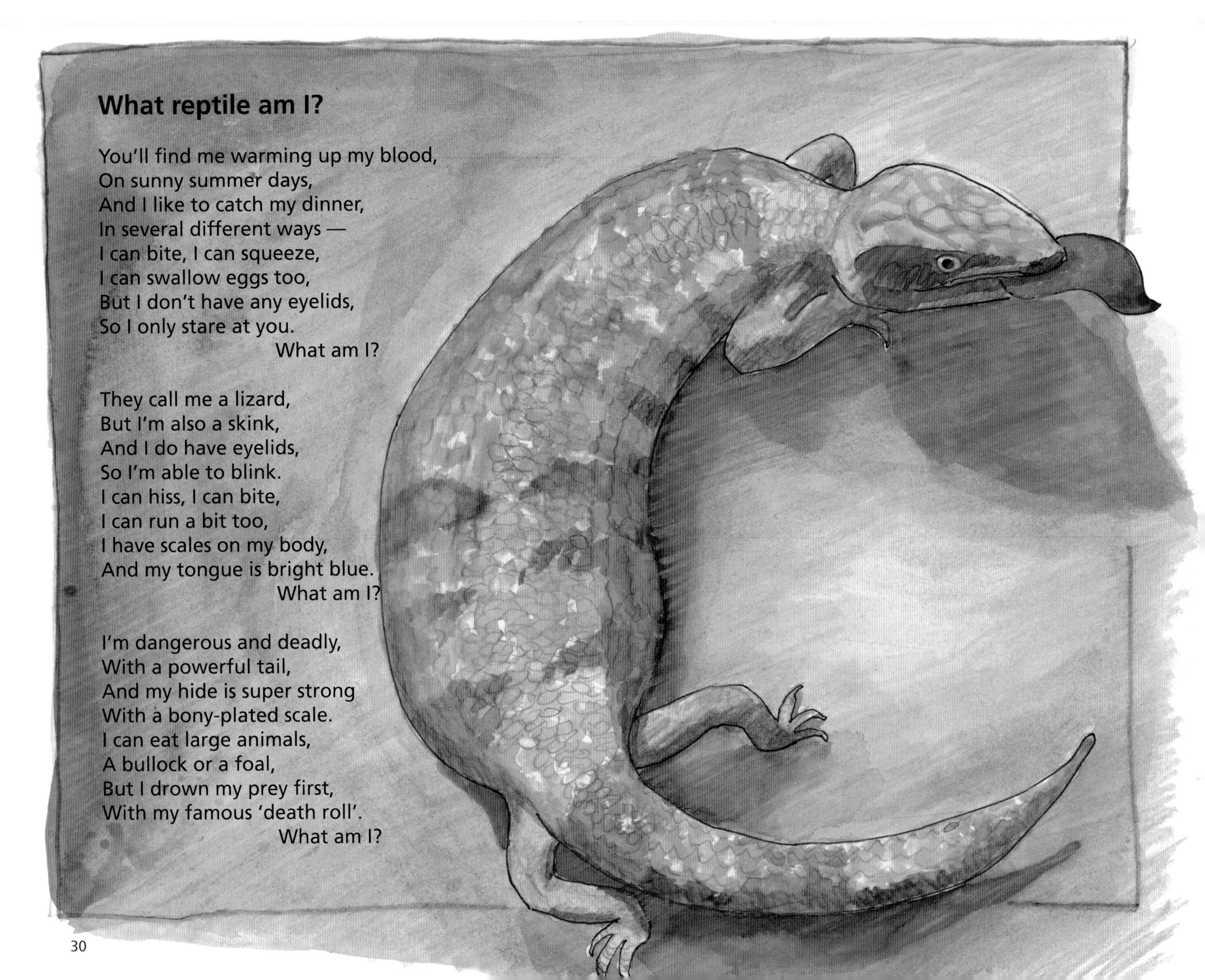

What reptile am I?

You'll find me warming up my blood,
On sunny summer days,
And I like to catch my dinner,
In several different ways —
I can bite, I can squeeze,
I can swallow eggs too,
But I don't have any eyelids,
So I only stare at you.
What am I?

They call me a lizard,
But I'm also a skink,
And I do have eyelids,
So I'm able to blink.
I can hiss, I can bite,
I can run a bit too,
I have scales on my body,
And my tongue is bright blue.
What am I?

I'm dangerous and deadly,
With a powerful tail,
And my hide is super strong
With a bony-plated scale.
I can eat large animals,
A bullock or a foal,
But I drown my prey first,
With my famous 'death roll'.
What am I?

Puppies

Puppies, puppies,
Everywhere,
Puppies here,
And puppies there.

Puppies barking,
Puppies biting,
Cheeky little
Puppies fighting.

Puppies running,
Puppies racing,
Chubby little
Puppies chasing.

In my face,
And on my hair.
Puppies, puppies,
Everywhere.

Cheeky dog

That dog is a cheeky one,
A sneaky try-to-eat-me one,
If I tease her she might come
And bite me on my precious … um,
Well, anyway, at least she's sleeping,
I can sneak past quietly creeping.

Wait a minute! There's a stick!
Maybe, if I'm really quick,
I could sort of … kind of … stroke her,
Whoops! I didn't mean to poke her.
Now she's getting to her feet,
And if she sees me I'm dead meat!
Lucky she's behind the fence.
Her teeth and eyes are sooo immense.

Help! She's trying to smash the gate,
She seems to be in quite a state,
She looks like she could eat a tiger,
I don't want to be inside 'er,
I'm not big enough to eat,
I'm mostly bone and not much meat.

Oh no! Look out! She's coming through,
She's bigger than a kangaroo,
Her mouth is massive and her jaws
Could crunch a tribe of dinosaurs.

Ow! She's got me in her grip
And any second flesh will rip,
Her teeth could bite a bus in two,
She'll swallow me with just one chew.

My number's up, my time has come,
Good-bye dad and good-bye mum,
See you cousins, sisters, brothers,
Uncles, aunts and all the others …

Here I go … it's dark in here,
Hey! Stop that tickling in my ear,
Just hurry up and make it quick.
I'm feeling kind of weak and sick.

Wait a minute! What's she doing?
She's not ripping flesh and chewing,
My clothes and hair are soaking wet,
This doggie's *licking* me to death!

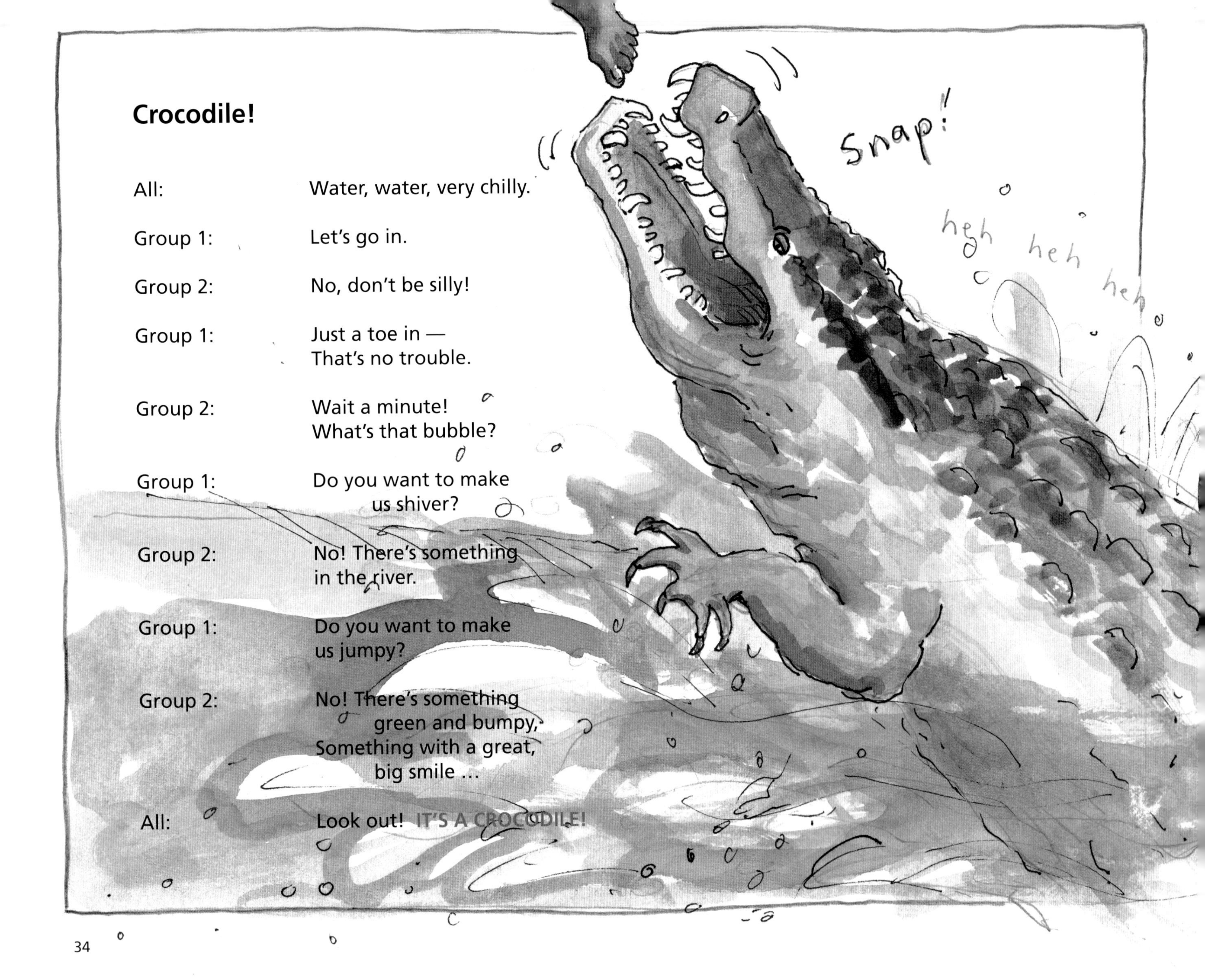

Crocodile!

All:	Water, water, very chilly.
Group 1:	Let's go in.
Group 2:	No, don't be silly!
Group 1:	Just a toe in — That's no trouble.
Group 2:	Wait a minute! What's that bubble?
Group 1:	Do you want to make us shiver?
Group 2:	No! There's something in the river.
Group 1:	Do you want to make us jumpy?
Group 2:	No! There's something green and bumpy, Something with a great, big smile …
All:	Look out! **IT'S A CROCODILE!**

Tissue rap

The symbol ^ indicates a clap.

When your nose is running like a ^ leaky tap,

You'd better grab yourself a tissue from the ^ tissue pack,

And when you've used your tissue from the ^ tissue pack,

You'd better not be thinking that you'll (ugh) put it back!

Now you take your tissue to the ^ tissue bin,

And you scrunch it up until it's (mm) mighty thin,

Then you step right back and you aim your shot,

And if it goes right in you know you're (mm) mighty hot.

So when your nose is running like a ^ leaky tap,

You'd better grab yourself a tissue from the ^ tissue pack,

And when you've used your tissue from the ^ tissue pack,

You'd better put your hands together for the ^ tissue rap.

Too many drunks

On Saturday,
We went to town,
But too many drunks,
Were walking around.

Too many drunks,
Annoying the crowd,
Swearing and staring,
And talking too loud.

Too many drunks,
All through the night,
Mumbling and grumbling,
And wanting to fight.

Too many drunks,
In too many places,
Too many hard times,
On too many faces.

Sad boys

"Sad boys are sniffing,"
Says the poster on the wall.
My brother is a sad boy,
And he never smiles at all.

He walks around,
His head is down,
A can is in his shirt,
He doesn't care
If people stare,
He lives in rags,
And sleeps on dirt.

My brother used to play all day,
And race his car across the clay,
He'd do the skids,
And all the kids,
Would jump in front and run away.

Sometimes he'd play footy
With the boys from Boggy Hole,
He'd grab the ball,
And dodge them all,
Before he scored a goal.

But now my brother's sniffing,
And he hasn't got a clue.
My brother is a sad boy,
And we all feel sad too.

Class rules OK!

"No teasing," said the teacher,
"No fighting in the school.
Be kind to all the little kids.
Remember, that's the rule."

"No swearing," said the teacher,
"Let's all have some fun.
Share the pencils, share the rubbers,
Share the toys with everyone."

"No fighting," said my brother,
"No mucking 'round in school.
'cos if you do, I'll follow you
And chuck you in the pool."

The Diamond Queens

We are the girls in the purple and green,
We're a score-makin', record-breakin' softball team.
We're meaner than we look and we look pretty mean,
But we call ourselves the Diamond Queens.

We played a team called the Western Crows,
From the sandhill country where the wild fig grows,
They had the roughest toughest players you've ever seen,
And they'd never even heard of the Diamond Queens.

The Crows drove down in their new white bus,
And they all sat inside looking down on us,
"They look like losers," said the captain of their team,
"And who's ever heard of the Diamond Queens?"

We went out to play on the eastern ground,
And everyone in camp came wandering down,
Even the boys from the footy team,
Came down to show support for the Diamond Queens.

The Crows batted first so we took our places,
Pitcher, backstop and all three bases,
Infield, outfield, everyone keen,
To show them why we're called the Diamond Queens.

Our pitcher wound up like a dynamo,
And sent a savage ball with an awesome throw,
The batter hit high but the ball went low,
"Strike one," cried the umpire. "Two to go."

The pitcher looked around with a gleam in her eye,
She still had a few more tricks to try,
She spat on the ball and let it fly,
"Strike two!" we heard the umpire cry.

The batter from the Crows was getting cross.
"I'll soon show you girls who's the boss!"
She smashed the ball with a smile on her face,
Straight to my cousin on second base.

Before too long all the Crows were out,
And the footy players began to shout,
"It's your turn girls," we heard them scream,
"Teach 'em not to mess with the Diamond Queens."

My cousin batted first and she took her place,
"Give this scrawny one heaps," cried the Crow on second base.
The pitcher looked around at her waiting team,
"Let's give 'em hell — these so-called Diamond Queens."

Then the pitcher sent a ball like a bullet from a gun,
And it nearly struck the umpire as she called, "Strike one!"
The second ball exploded like dynamite,
"Strike two," yelled the umpire and her face turned white.

My cousin faced up for the final throw,
And the backstop whispered, "Don't you know?
You can't beat the Crows in your wildest dreams,
No one's even heard of the Diamond Queens."

Then the pitcher let the third ball fly,
My cousin swung her bat and smashed it high,
Up, up, it went through the clear blue sky,
"Home run!" we heard the big boys cry.

"Fluke", snarled the backstop and her face looked mean,
As we watched my cousin pick up steam,
She hit the plate with a mighty scream,
"YEEES!" went the crowd, "GO THE DIAMOND QUEENS".

Then our girls faced the pitcher one by one,
And every single player hit a big home run,
Till the score was nil to seventeen,
When the Western Crows played the Diamond Queens.

The Crows were very quiet when the game was done,
And they climbed on their big bus one by one.
"Excuse me," said my cousin to the captain of their team,
"NOW you've heard of the Diamond Queens."

My sister's salary

Today my sister got her pay,
She cashed her cheque and straight away
She gave me money for the store,
$50 — maybe more!

First I told my dear old gran,
Who said, "You take your brother's hand,
And don't forget to buy some meat,
We haven't got a thing to eat."

Next I raced up to the school,
To get a drink (the water's cool).
"Wait for me," my brother cried,
And so we went on side by side.

Then we passed my favourite friend,
Who didn't have a cent to spend.
"I'll share with you. Come on, let's go!"
So off we went — three in a row.

Soon my friend said, "There's the bus,
My little niece might come with us."
And so we waited for one more,
Then off we went again — all four.

Next my cousin Mabeline
Came running up to join our team,
Past the hospital we ran,
All five together — hand in hand.

And long before we reached the store,
Another dozen kids or more,
Had joined with us along the way,
To help me spend my sister's pay.

Everyone picked things to buy,
A sausage roll, an apple pie,
A drink, some chips, a tin of meat,
For everyone, a little treat.

I paid for everybody's stuff,
And luckily there was enough,
And still enough to get some meat,
Three little chops for us to eat.

Three little chops was all we had,
But still it made me really glad,
To spend my sister's salary,
On all my friends and family.

The footy game

We had a footy game one day,
And all the boys went out to play,
Through the camp, they spread the news —
"Green Birds play the Kangaroos!"

The dads and aunts and all the mums,
Said, "Let's go down and watch the fun,
We don't know who will win or lose,
When Green Birds play the Kangaroos."

The Kangaroos were fat but tall,
The Birds were tough but they were small,
They faced each other two by two,
The Green Birds and the Kangaroos.

The whistle blew, the teams ran out,
The crowd began to cheer and shout,
"Come on the Greens!" "Come on the Blues!"
"Green Birds play the Kangaroos!"

Up the field the players tore,
And Roos tried hard to make a score.
A big boy kicked but lost his shoes!
When Green Birds played the Kangaroos.

The score was level — twenty all,
When Green Birds jumped and won the ball,
The rover kicked and put one through,
When Green Birds played the Kangaroos.

The crowd went wild on every side,
"Up the Mighty Birds," they cried.
"Green and yellow, we love you!"
When Green Birds played the Kangaroos.

The Roos were big but they were weak,
They tried to fight, they tried to cheat,
The crowd began to hiss and boo,
When Green Birds played the Kangaroos.

The Green Bird boys played tough but clean,
The showed respect for the gold and green,
With strength and pride their colours flew,
When Green Birds played the Kangaroos.

At last the final whistle blew,
With Birds ahead by twenty-two,
All through the camp they spread the news —
Green Birds **THRASHED** the Kangaroos.

Ozzie the Mozzie

I'm Ozzie the Mozzie
Do you remember me?
You donated blood this morning
And you gave so generously.
If I'm feeling peckish
Then I might drop in for tea,
Let's make a date, but if I'm late
Please …
don't wait up for me.

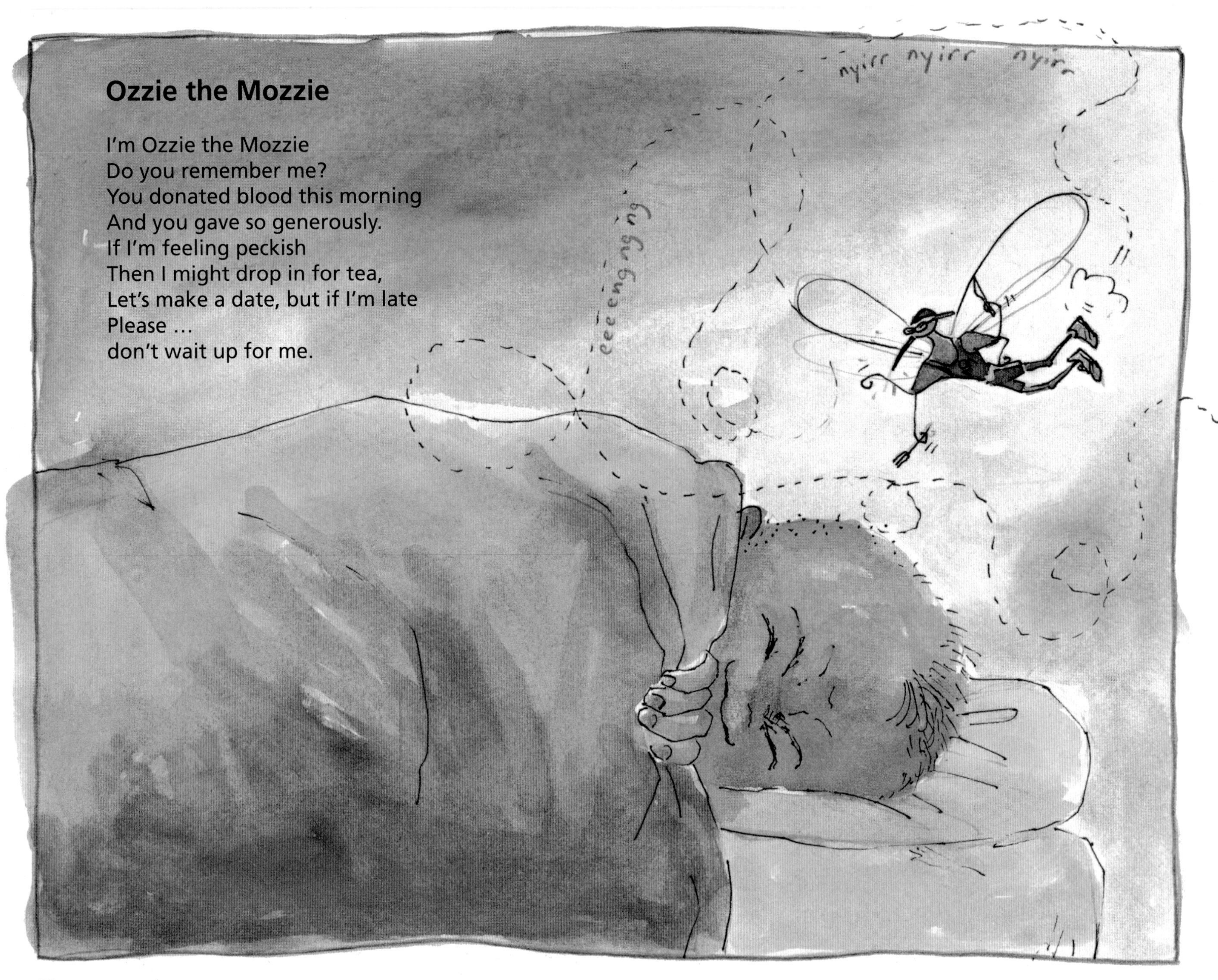

Reconciliation

Black fella
White fella
Dark fella
Light fella.

Different outside
Same within
Same blood
Different skin.

Same planet
Same sun
We are many
We are one.

Jill McDougall has lived and taught for many years in Australian Indigenous communities, from Palm Island in the east of Australia to the Great Sandy Desert in the west. She began writing for Aboriginal children in order to provide classroom reading material which reflected the daily experiences of her students. Jill has written over 20 books for children. Find out more about Jill at www.jillmcdougall.com.au.

Jenny Taylor has lived in Central Australia since 1994 and has worked with artists and families in a number of Aboriginal communities. She currently works in adult education, at the Institute for Aboriginal Development in Alice Springs, and maintains her own art practice.

Aboriginal Studies Press
Paperback edition, 2008
First published in hardback, 2000

Aboriginal Studies Press
is the publishing arm of the
Australian Institute of Aboriginal
and Torres Strait Islander Studies.
GPO Box 553, Canberra, ACT 2601
Phone: (61 2) 6246 1183
Fax: (61 2) 6261 4288
Email: asp@aiatsis.gov.au
Web: www.aiatsis.gov.au/aboriginal_studies_press

National Library of Australia
Cataloguing-In-Publication data:

Author: McDougall, Jill, 1951-
Title: Anna the goanna : and other poems / author, Jill McDougall.
Publisher: Canberra : Aboriginal Studies Press, 2008.
ISBN: 978 0 85575 616 1 (pbk.)
Notes: Previously published: Barn-Barn Barlala, Why the emu can't fly, Kangaroo who wanted to be People and How Crows became black.
Includes index.
Subjects: Aboriginal Australians — Juvenile Poetry. Children's poetry, Australian. Australia — Juvenile poetry.
Dewey Number: A821.4

Printed in China by Phoenix Offset & Bookbuilders